ŠEVČÍK

VIOLIN STUDIES

OPUS 2 PART 2

SCHOOL OF BOWING
TECHNIQUE

SCHULE DER
BOGENTECHNIK

ÉCOLE DE LA TECHNIQUE
DE L'ARCHET

BOSWORTH

BOE005051

ISMN: M2016 40778

Music settting by Musonix

Cover design: Miranda Harvey

Cover picture: The Farmouth Stradivari, Cremona 1692 (Antonio Stradivari)

© Christie's Images Ltd. 2001

This edition © 2001 Bosworth & Company Ltd.

Sales and Hire:

Hal Leonard Europe Distribution Centre,

Newmarket Road,

Bury St Edmunds,

Suffolk IP33 3YB

www.halleonard.com

Die Anzahl der möglichen Kombinationen von Stricharten und Bogenführungen ist unbegrenzt. Ševčíks „Schule der Bogentechnik" ermöglicht das Einüben der grundlegenden Stricharten und Bogentechniken durch systematische und sinnvolle Anordnung der Übungseinheiten.

Dabei wird es einfacher, wenn man beim Üben ein paar grundsätzliche Dinge immer wieder überprüft:

1. Auf welchem Bogenabschnitt beginnt und endet der Strich?
2. Wie nah ist der Bogen am Steg? Werden alle Stricharten im gleichen Abstand zum Steg ausgeführt, oder muss man bei manchen Stricharten näher an den Steg heran?
3. Wie steht's mit dem Bogentempo: ist der Strich gleichmäßig schnell, oder ist ein Tempowechsel zwischen Auf- und Abstrich gefordert?
4. Wie hoch ist der Bogendruck auf die Saiten? Soll er gleichbleibend sein oder variieren?
5. Wieviel Bogenhaar macht den Ton am rundesten? Soll immer mit vollem Bogenhaar gestrichen werden oder führt eine Teilung zum erwünschten Ausdruck im Ton?

Während die Bogenrichtung immer genau beachtet werden soll, darf bei der Tongebung mehr auf den musikalischen und künstlerischen Aspekt geachtet werden als nur auf die pure mechanische Exaktheit. Beim Durchmessen des ganzen dynamischen Raums von *p* bis *f* muss man genau hinhören, welche Töne man mit welchem Bogenstrich dem Instrument entlockt. Es ist erstrebenswert, klangreine und ausdrucksstarke Wendungen zu spielen.

Umso exakter und konsequenter die Stricharten eingeübt werden, umso größer wird der Vorrat an verfügbaren Stricharten, die man wo immer angebracht einsetzen kann. Das Vom-Blatt-Lesen schult, und wenn spezielle Wendungen in einem Stück vorkommen, bleibt die den Spielfluss vernichtende Überraschung aus, wenn man auf bekannte Bogentechniken für bestimmte Wendungen zurückgreifen kann. Der Standard ist beim Beginn der Einübung eines Stückes einfach höher und das Erarbeiten wird deutlich leichter fallen.

Wiederholung.

Das effektivste Vorgehen ist, zunächst immer nur einen Takt oder eine übung zu erarbeiten, aber dies auf so viele Arten wie möglich. Mit Aufstrich beginnend oder mit Abstrich; mit wenig Bogenstrich am Frosch, mit der Mitte des Bogens oder mit der Spitze; mit mehr Bogen in der unteren und der oberen Hälfte oder in der Mitte; mit ganzem Bogen; in dichtestem *legato*; mit Akzenten als *martellato* oder *staccato* an den Stellen, wo Punkte über den Noten dies erfordern; in der unteren Bogenhälfte die kurzen Töne mit Abheben des Bogens von der Saite mit unterschiedlich deutlichem *spiccato* — rundes und gesangliches *spiccato* mit mehr Längs — und weniger Höhenbewegung, kürzeres und schärferes *spiccato* mit umgekehrter

Aufteilung von Höhe und Länge. Beim Ausprobieren der verschiedenen Bogentechniken gewinnt man an Kontrolle über den Bogenarm und erkennt die Möglichkeiten, mit dem Bogenstrich Farbe und Dynamik des Tons zu bestimmen.

Bogenstellung.

Auf dem Abschnitt zwischen Steg und Griffbrett wird der Bogen auf die Saite aufgesetzt. In der ersten Lage erscheint die G-Saite zu hart, wenn man zu nah am Steg streicht, die E-Saite dagagen wirkt in der nähe des Griffbretts gestrichen zu weich.

Zur Veranschaulichung unterteilen wir diesen Abschnitt auf der Geige in 5 Punkte, wobei Punkt 1 nah am Steg, Punkt 3 in der Mitte und Punkt 5 am Griffbrett liegt.

Von musikalischen Notwendigkeiten abgesehen, liegt der optimale Berührungspunkt grob an folgenden Punkten:

Dies gilt grundsätzlich gleichermaßen für leere und gegriffene Töne. In Band II, Nr. 16 muss die Bogenstellung der verwendeten Saite entsprechend wie angegeben verändert werden um einen optimalen Ton zu bekommen:

Übergänge zwischen Bogenstrichen.

So wie man die Qualität des Tons durch ständiges Hineinhören und Verbessern optimiert, müssen auch die Übergänge zwischen den Bogenstrichen fortwährend überprüft werden in Bezug auf enge und gleichmäßige Bindung. Eine durchgängig gleiche Bogengeschwindigkeit ist besonders beim Strichwechsel wichtig.

Fließende Saitenwechsel.

Um einen fließenden Übergang ohne unerwünschte Akzente von einer Saite zur anderen zu erreichen, muss dieser Wechsel schon während des letzten Tons auf der „alten" Saite vorbereitet werden. Der Bogen wird schon langsam auf die „neue" Saite zubewegt. Das Thema in Band I, Nr. 6 ist ein typisches Beispiel für zahlreiche Saitenwechsel:

*Während des leeren
A auf die D-Saite
zubewegen*

*In der Nähe der D-Saite
bleiben während des
Tons auf der G-Saite*

Bei mehreren Wechseln zwischen 2 Saiten kann der Bogen fast in
gleicher Stellung gehalten werden wie bei Doppelgriffen. Im
folgenden Beispiel aus Band III, Nr. 29 (Var. 7b) verbleibt der
Bogen fast auf der E-Saite während die A-Saite gestrichen wird,
ebenso wie beim Spielen auf der A-Saite der Bogen in unmittelbarer
Nähe zur E-Saite gehalten wird.

*Bogen nah
an der E-Saite*   *Bogen nah
an der A-Saite*

Verschiebung der Bogenposition beim Saitenwechsel.

Beim Überspringen von einer oder zwei Saiten beim Wechsel muss
der Bogen auf der „alten" Saite langsam in Richtung des für die
neue Saite optimalen Punktes (Punkte 1-5 zwischen Steg und
Griffbrett, s.o.) bewegt werden. Der Ton auf der „neuen" Saite wird
dann auf halbem Weg begonnen und dann zum optimalen Punkt
hingeführt.

*Beginnt näher am Griffbrett
als üblich, aber näher am
Steg als sein Vorgänger*

*Beginnt näher am Steg
als üblich, aber näher am
Griffbrett als sein Vorgänger*

Gleichzeitiges Greifen mit 2 Fingern.

Beim Spielen von Doppelgriff-Übungen (z.B. Band III, Nr. 29) ist es
einfacher, die Finger der linken Hand gleichzeitig — nicht
nacheinander — aufzusetzen.

*Nur die untere
Note spielen*

*Nur die obere
Note spielen*

Markierung der Übungen.

Es müssen nicht alle Übungen der Reihe nach abgearbeitet werden.
Es ist übersichtlich, die gespielten Übungen zu markieren. So kann
man die Übungen je nach Bedarf und Interesse auswählen ohne zu
befürchten, dass wichtige Übungen unberücksichtigt bleiben.
Mehrfach wieder aufgegriffene Übungen können auch mehrfach
markiert werden. So weiß man immer, wie der Stand der Dinge ist.

SIMON FISCHER
London, 2000
Übersetzung: D. Fratz

Otakar Ševčík Opus 2

The number of possible combinations of bow strokes and bowing patterns is endless. Ševčík's *School of Bowing Technique* makes it possible for the principal strokes and patterns to be studied in a way that is systematic and easily organised.

Ask yourself a series of simple questions while working on any bow stroke or bowing pattern:

1. Exactly where in the bow does the stroke begin and end?
2. How close is the bow to the bridge? Is each stroke the same, or should some strokes be closer to the bridge than others?
3. How fast is the bow? Is the speed even, or is it fast–slow, slow–fast, fast–slow–fast, etc.?
4. How heavy is the weight of the bow into the string? Is it even, or heavy–light, light–heavy, heavy–light–heavy, etc.?
5. How much hair gives the best tone or feel in the stroke? Does it stay the same, or should it begin tilted and then change to full hair, etc.?

While strictly observing the directions for bow division, approach the variations musically and artistically, rather than purely mechanically. Playing at all dynamics from *p* to *f*, listen carefully in order to catch every single sound that comes out of the instrument. Strive to make the bowing patterns sound both beautiful and expressive.

The better and more exactly the strokes are designed, the greater the player's repertoire of strokes which are ready for use whenever required. Sight-reading improves as particular patterns become familiar and no longer cause surprise when encountered for the first time. The standard at the beginning of learning a piece is therefore much higher.

Repetition.

An effective approach is to practise only one bar or variation at a time, but to do so in as many different ways as possible. Begin up-bow, begin down-bow; use little bow entirely at the frog, at the middle, at the point; then more bow in the lower half, in the middle, in the upper half; then whole bows; play *legato*; play with accents. In the upper half use *martelé* or *staccato* for the dotted notes; in the lower half play the dotted notes *spiccato*, experimenting with different characters of stroke — rounded and singing *spiccato* (using more length and less height), shorter and crisper *spiccato* (more height and less length). By exploring a variety of different articulations, the bow arm gains greatly in control and in its range of colour and attack.

Point-of-contact.

The area between the bridge and the fingerboard is called the 'point-of-contact'. In first position, the G string feels too hard under the bow if you play too near to the bridge. The E string feels too soft if you play too near to the fingerboard.

Subdivide the point-of-contact into different 'tracks' or 'soundpoints', so that Soundpoint 1 is close to the bridge, Soundpoint 3 is in the middle, and Soundpoint 5 is close to the fingerboard.

Musical considerations apart, the optimum places to bow the open strings are roughly as follows:

The same basic proportions then apply to stopped notes on each string. In Volume II, No. 16, the bow needs to move further from or closer to the bridge depending on the string:

Connexions between strokes.

As well as listening for the tone quality of individual bow strokes, concentrate on the connexions *between* strokes, binding them together smoothly and evenly. In particular avoid increasing the bow speed or pressure just before changing direction.

Smooth string crossings.

In order to cross smoothly from one string to another, without accent, the bow must begin to move to the new string *while* playing the note on the previous string. The theme in Volume I, No. 6 is a typical example that contains many string crossings:

When crossing continuously between two strings, the bow can stay almost on the same level as when playing them as a double stop. In the following example from Volume III, No. 29 (variant 7b), the bow can almost touch the E string while playing the A string, and can almost touch the A string while playing the E string:

Gaining and losing bow on string crossing.

When playing variations that skip one or two strings, as in Volume III, No. 30, notice the changing contact point of the hair with the string.

Putting fingers down together.

When playing variations on a theme of double-stops, e.g. Volume III, No. 29, put the left fingers down at the same time rather than placing first one finger, and then the other finger.

Keeping track.

Mark with a tick every bar that you work on. A tick does not have to mean that the section is 'perfect', only that you have practised it. You can always practise it again on other occasions, marking it again each time. Keeping a record in this way means that you can play the variations in any order and can go directly to whatever seems particularly relevant or interesting at the time; it also means that you always know what you have already played.

SIMON FISCHER
London, 2000

Le nombre de combinaisons possibles des tenues d'archet et des formules de coups d'archet est infini. *L'Ecole de la technique de l'archet* de Ševčík fournit la possibilité d'étudier les principales tenues et formules de coups d'archet de façon systématique et facile à organiser.

Posez-vous cette série de questions simples lors de votre travail de tout coup d'archet ou tenue d'archet:

1 A quel endroit précis de l'archet commence et se termine le coup d'archet?

2 A quelle distance se trouve d'archet du chevalet? Tous les coups d'archets sont-ils les mêmes ou certains devraient-ils être plus proches du chevalet que d'autres?

3 A quelle vitesse s'effectue le coup d'archet? La rapidité de chaque coup d'archet est-elle égale ou varie-t-elle selon un schéma rapide–lent, lent–rapide, rapide–lent–rapide, etc.?

4 Quelle est la pression de l'archet sur la corde? Est-elle égale ou variable: forte–légère, légère–forte, forte–légère–forte,etc.?

5 Quelle tension du crin donne la meilleure sonorité ou procure le coup d'archet le plus aisé? Reste-t-elle égale ou doit-elle varier de plus à moins relâchée, etc.?

Tout en observant scrupuleusement les indications de division de l'archet, abordez les exercices et leurs variantes avec musicalité et sens artistique et non en pure mécanique. Jouez dans toutes les nuances du *p* au *f* en vous écoutant attentivement de manière à saisir toute la diversité des sons produits par l'instrument. Efforcez-vous d'exécuter les formules de coups d'archet avec expression et une belle sonorité.

Plus les coups d'archet sont travaillés avec exactitude, plus l'interprète enrichit son répertoire de coups d'archet prêts à être utilisés si nécessaire. Sa lecture à vue s'améliore tandis qu'il se familiarise avec certaines formules lui évitant la surprise de les rencontrer pour la première fois. Son niveau d'apprentissage s'élève d'autant.

Répétition.
Un travail efficace consiste à n'aborder qu'une mesure ou une variante à la fois mais de toutes les manières possibles. Attaquez en tirant puis en poussant sur l'archet; utilisez peu d'archet entièrement à la hausse, au milieu, à la pointe; puis plus d'archet à la partie inférieure, au milieu, à la partie supérieure; puis tout l'archet; jouez sur la corde avec le legato le plus uni; effectuez des accents en pratiquant le *martellato* ou le *staccato* pour les notes piquées; à la moitié inférieure, jouez les notes piquées en relevant de la corde avec différentes sortes de *spiccato* — *spiccato* rond et chantant avec plus de longueur et moins de hauteur, *spiccato* bref et sec avec plus de hauteur et moins de longueur. Par le travail de

différentes articulations, le bras tenant l'archet acquiert une grande maîtrise ouvrant un large éventail de couleurs et d'attaques.

Point de contact.
L'espace compris entre le chevalet et la touche s'appelle le 'point de contact'. Dans la première position, la corde de *sol* s'avère trop dure sous l'archet si on la joue trop près du chevalet et la corde de *mi* trop souple si on la joue trop près de la touche.

Divisez le point de contact en plusieurs 'plages' ou 'points de production de son', de façon que la plage 1 se situe près du chevalet, la plage 3 au milieu et la plage 5 près de la touche.

En dehors de toute considération musicale, les meilleurs emplacements des coups d'archets sur les cordes à vide se situent à peu près ainsi:

Les mêmes proportions de base s'appliquent alors aux notes pincées sur chaque corde. Dans l'exercice no. 16 du volume II, l'archet doit s'éloigner ou se rapprocher du chevalet en fonction de chaque corde:

Articulations entre les coups d'archet.
De même que vous prêtez attention à la qualité de son de chaque coup d'archet, concentrez-vous sur les articulations *entre* les coups d'archets afin que ceux-ci soient reliés de façon lisse et égale. Evitez, en particulier, d'augmenter la rapidité ou la pression de l'archet juste avant de changer de direction.

Passage égal d'une corde à l'autre.
Pour passer sans à-coups ni accent d'une corde à l'autre, on commence à déplacer l'archet vers la nouvelle corde *tout en* jouant la note sur la corde précédente. Le thème de l'exercice no. 6 du volume I contient de nombreux passages d'une corde à l'autre caractéristiques:

Déplacement vers la corde de ré tout en jouant le la à vide

Maintien près de la corde de ré tout en jouant la note sur la corde de sol

Ne jouer que la note supérieure

Ne jouer que la note inférieure

Lors de passages constants d'une corde à l'autre, l'archet garde à peu près la même position que pour l'exécution des doubles cordes. Dans l'exemple suivant extrait du no. 29 du volume III (variante 7b), l'archet peut presque toucher la corde de *mi* tout en jouant la corde de *la* et peut presque toucher la corde de *la* tout en jouant la corde de *mi*:

Archet près de la corde de mi   *Archet près de la corde de la*

Augmentation et diminution d'archet lors des passages de cordes.

Observez le changement de point de contact du crin sur la corde pour jouer des exercices dans lesquels on saute une ou deux cordes, comme dans le no. 30 du volume III.

Attaquer plus bas sur le crin qu'à la fin de la note précédente

Attaquer plus haut qu'à la fin de la note précédente

Abaisser les doigts ensemble.

Dans les variantes d'un exercice en doubles cordes, par exemple dans le no. 29 du volume III, abaissez simultanément les doigts de la main gauche plutôt que de les placer l'un après l'autre.

Garder des traces de son travail.

Marquez d'une croix chaque mesure étudiée. Une croix ne signifie pas nécessairement que la section est exécutee 'parfaitement' mais seulement que vous l'avez travaillée. Vous pourrez toujours y revenir, en la marquant à chaque fois. Garder de telles traces vous permettra de jouer les exercices dans n'importe quel ordre et de vous concentrer directement sur ceux qui vous paraîtront les plus indiqués ou intéressants à un certain moment tout en sachant à tout instant ce que vous avez déjà joué.

SIMON FISCHER
London, 2000
Traduction: Agnès Ausseur

La quantità di possibili combinazioni di arcate e di colpi d'arco è veramente inesauribile. *La Scuola della Tecnica dei Colpi d'arco* di Ševčík rende possibile lo studio dei colpi d'arco più importanti in una maniera sistematica e ben organizzata.

Durante lo studio di qualsiasi colpo d'arco è bene porsi una serie di semplici domande:

1   Qual'è il punto esatto dell'arco dove il contatto con la corda incomincia e finisce?

2   Quanto dista l'arco dal ponticello? Le arcate sono tutte uguali, o alcune possono essere più vicine al ponticello daltre?

3   Quanto è veloce l'arco? La velocità è costante o cambia da veloce–piano, piano–veloce, veloce–piano–veloce, ecc.?

4   Quanto è pesante l'arco e qual'è la pressione effettuata sulla corda? E' una pressione costante, o cambia da pesante–leggero, leggero–pesante, pesante–leggero-pesante?

5   Qual'è la quantità ideale di crini per ottenere un buon suono? Tale quantità rimane invariata o l'arco deve essere prima in posizione inclinata per poi mutare posizione onde usare tutti i crini ecc.?

Unitamente all'osservanza rigorosa delle direzioni per la divisione delle arcate, si affrontino le variazioni con senso musicale e artistico, invece di attenersi a esercizi puramente meccanici. Quando si suonano tutte le dinamiche da *p* a *f*, ascoltare con attenzione per poter cogliere ciascun singolo suono proveniente dallo strumento. Nell'esecuzione degli esercizi si faccia tutto il possibile per ottenere un suono bello ed espressivo.

Una maggiore accuratezza e perfezione contenuta nei colpi d'arco studiati rende più ampio il repertorio e l'esperienza del violinista, che avrà pronti per l'uso questi modelli in qualsiasi momento se ne presenti l'occasione. La lettura a prima vista migliora in quanto si ha una maggiore dimestichezza con specifici tipi di colpi d'arco e perciò non si è colti di sorpresa quando si incontrano per la prima volta. Il grado di conoscenza è perciò molto più avanzato quando si affronta un brano nuovo.

Ripetizione.

Per un approccio efficace, si studi una sola battuta o variazione per volta, facendolo però in una multiplicità di modi diversi. Cominciare con arcata in su, cominciare con arcata in giù; usare poco arco completamente al tallone, nel mezzo, alla punta; poi si aggiunga più arco nella metà inferiore, nel mezzo, nella metà superiore; poi tutto l'arco; suonare sulla corda il più legato possibile; suonare con accenti, usando martellato o staccato per le note puntate; nella metà inferiore dell'arco suonare i punti via dalla corda con vari tipi di spiccato — spiccato rotondo e cantabile con più lunghezza e meno altezza, spiccato corto e secco con più altezza e meno lunghezza. Esplorando una varietà di articolazioni diverse

aumenta di molto il controllo del braccio destro e la varietà di colori e attacchi a disposizione.

Punto di contatto.

L'area tra il ponticello e la tastiera si chiama 'punto di contatto'. In prima posizione, se si suona troppo vicino al ponticello, la corda *Sol* si sente troppo tesa sotto l'arco. Se si suona troppo vicino alla tastiera, la corda *Mi* si sente troppo debole.

Suddividere il punto di contatto in diverse 'sezioni' o 'punti di sonorità' in modo che il punto di sonorità 1 è vicino al ponticello, punto di sonorità 3 è nel mezzo, ed il punto di sonorità 5 è vicino alla tastiera.

Se mettiamo da parte le considerazioni musicali, i punti perfetti in cui poggiare l'arco sulle corde vuote sono più o meno le seguenti:

Le stesse proporzioni basilari sono poi applicate alle note suonate solo con dita. Nel Volume II, n. 16, dipendendo dalla corda in uso, l'arco deve essere spostato più lontano o più vicino al ponticello.

Cambio d'arcata uniforme.

Unitamente all'ascolto delle qualità tonali e individuali dei colpi d'arco, si prega di concentrarsi sulla connessione esistente tra un colpo d'arco e l'altro, unendoli insieme in modo legato e costante. In modo particolare si eviti l'aumento della velocità del colpo d'arco o della pressione prima del cambiamento di direzione.

Cambiamento di corda uniforme.

Per poter cambiare direzione in modo uniforme tra una corda e l'altra, e senza accenti, l'arco deve incominciare a spostarsi verso la nuova corda mentre si suona la nota sulla corda precedente. Il tema nel Volume I, n. 6 è un esempio tipico contente molti cambiamenti di corde.

Quando alternate le due corde continuamente, l'arco può rimanere quasi allo stesso livello di come quando si suona su doppia corda. Nel seguente esempio tratto dal Volume III, n. 29 (variante 7b) l'arco può quasi toccare la corda *Mi* mentre suona la corda *La*, e può quasi toccare la corda *La* mentre suona la corda *Mi*.

Guadagnare o perdere lunghezza dell'arco nei cambi di corda (distribuzione).

Quando si suonano variazioni che saltano una o due corde, come si vede nel Volume III, n. 30, si noti il cambiamento del punto di contatto tra i crini e la corda.

Appoggiare le dita sulla tastiera contemporaneamente.

Quando si suonano variazioni su un tema di doppie corde, come quelle illustrate nel Volume III, n. 29, appoggiare contemporaneamente le dita della mano sinistra invece di posare giù prima un dito, e poi l'altro.

Tenere nota del materiale studiato.

Notare ogni battuta studiata. L'annotazione non vuol dire necessariamente che la sezione sia 'perfetta' ma solo che è stata studiata. Potete sempre ripassarla di nuovo in un'altra occasione, ed ogni volta vanno notate le battute studiate. Tenendo nota in questo modo significa che è possibile suonare le variazioni in qualsiasi ordine ed è inoltre possibile puntare direttamente su ciò che è particolarmente rilevante o interessante in quel momento; vuol dire anche che siete sempre al corrente di ciò che avete già suonato.

SIMON FISCHER
London, 2000
Traduzione: Anna Maggio

VORWORT DES HERAUSGEBERS

Die Neuausgabe eines Werkes, das auf seinem Gebiet einen „Klassiker" darstellt, darf man nicht auf die leichte Schulter nehmen. Ein Technik-Handbuch vom Rang der Ševčík Violinstudien stellt dabei eine große Herausforderung dar. Der Herausgeber sieht sich dabei nicht nur einer völlig anderen, neuen Generation gegenüber. Auch die Verantwortung gegenüber aktuellen Entwicklungen und Strömungen ist in Einklang zu bringen mit dem Erhalt der wichtigen Eigenheiten des Werkes; es kommt auf eine gute Balance zwischen Erneuern und Erhalten an!

Die Originalausgabe erschien anfang der 20er Jahre. Sie trägt inzwischen deutliche Spuren ihres Alters sowohl im äußeren Erscheinungsbild von Notenstich und Seitenbild als auch in der Wortwahl. Dass das Werk bis heute überdauert hat, beweist die Schlüssigkeit des großen Rahmens, in dem das Werk konzipiert ist. Mein Ziel war als, seine attraktiven und bestens erprobten Bestandteile und Grundzüge zu erhalten und Abhilfe zu schaffen, wo der Originaltext über die Jahre mehr oder weniger ungebräuchlich geworden ist.

Die meisten deutschen Abkürzungen sind beibehalten worden. Trotzdem sind einige wenige Termini ausgemustert worden im Interesse einer einheitlichen Stilistik der Bände untereinander.

Die sorgfältigen Übersetzungen der Originalausgabe zu Artikulation und Bogentechnik waren nicht immer glücklich. Es wurde versucht, aus dem Deutschen heraus mit beinahe wörtlichen Übersetzungen ins Englische, Französische, Italienische, Tschechische und Russische die Ševčík'schen formulierungen herüberzuretten. (Kurioserweise sind italienische Standardbegriffe, wie z.B. *staccato*, aus dem deutschen Text mit einem anderen Wort ins Italienische zurückübertragen worden.) Dies führt nicht nur zu konstruiert wirkenden Formulierungen, es irritiert auch sachlich.

So wurde in dem Bemühen, die Texte möglichst authentisch zu Übertragen bisweilen genau das Gegenteil erreicht, indem der Wort-für-Wort-Übersetzung der Vorzug vor einer sinnechten Übersetzung gegeben wurde.

Um hier eine klare Linie zu ziehen, wurde auf internationale Standardausdrücke zurückgegriffen. So muss z.B. *spiccato* ohne die deutsche Übersetzung „geworfen" auskommen, auch die italienische Übersetzung „sciolto balzato" ist nicht gebräuchlich und also entfernt worden; *jeté* ist nicht übersetzt zu „werfend", „thrown", „jerked", „balzato" oder „di rimbalzo"; *saltando* steht auch für die überflüssigen Übersetzungen „springend", „hopping", „sautillé", „saltellato" und „saltato"; *volante* für „fliegend", „flying", „volant"; *martellato* für „gehämmert", „hammered", „martelé"; und *staccato* für „gestoßen", „chopped" oder „picchettato (secco)". (Unglücklicherweise verwirrt die alte Ausgabe hier auch noch mit dem Begriff „detaché".) Ohne Zweifel lässt diese Liste die — unbeabsichtigten — feinen Bedeutungsunterschiede erkennen zwischen den gebräuchlichen Fachbegriffen und den hölzernen Übersetzungen.

Letztlich befleißigt sich die Ausgabe einer modernisierten Notenschrift und eines ansprechenden, zeitgemäßen Layouts, womit eine bessere Lesbarkeit der Ševčík-Übungen erreicht wird, so dass man die Studien einfach lieber in Angriff nimmt. Einige offensichtliche Fehler wurden beseitigt und die Übungsanweisungen gestrafft und sprachlich aktualisiert.

MILLAN SACHANIA
Shepperton, England, 2000
Übersetzung: D. Fratz

Editorial Preface

Preparing a new edition of a work which is a classic in its field is a task that cannot be lightly undertaken. A manual of technique as prestigious as the Sevčík Violin Studies presents its own challenges. In renovating it, the editor must not only consider new and potential users of the work; there is also a responsibility to relieve existing, experienced users of needless fuss and discomfort in 'up-grading' to the new edition. This calls for a balanced approach, one which blends innovation with conservation.

The previous edition first appeared in print at the beginning of the twentieth century. It showed signs of its age both in its notational style and in the quality of the engraving and image. Yet its durability attested to the strength of its broader conception. My aim has thus been to retain its most attractive and well-established features whilst remedying those defects which detracted from its usefulness. Accordingly, most of the German abbreviations of the former edition have been retained. A few, however, have been jettisoned in the interests of stylistic consistency between the volumes.

In its quest for linguistic parity, the former edition painstakingly translated much of the terminology denoting bowing styles and articulation. Generally starting from the German, it supplied equivalents in English, French, Italian, Czech, and Russian. (Curiously, though, the older edition often reserved standard Italian terms such as 'staccato' for the directions in the languages *other* than Italian; in these cases, the Italian directions deployed an alternative Italian word or phrase.) This practice served not only to clutter the text, but also to confuse. For though the intention was almost certainly to provide the closest equivalent in the language concerned (borne out by the consistency of the 'translations'), inevitably the translations sometimes carried different nuances of meaning from those suggested by the original concepts. In the interests of clarity, the present edition uses standard international terminology. *Spiccato* appears without the attendant German 'geworfen' and the alternative Italian 'sciolto balzato'; *jeté*, without the attendant 'werfend', 'thrown', 'jerked', 'balzato', 'di rimbalzo'; *saltando* is given in place of 'springend', 'hopping', 'sautillé', 'saltellato', 'saltato'; *volante* for 'fliegend', 'flying', 'volant'; *martellato* for 'gehämmert', 'hammered', 'martelé'; and *staccato* for 'abgestoßen', 'chopped', and 'picchettato (secco)'. (Incidentally, the previous edition sometimes confused 'détaché' with 'staccato'.) Doubtless the preceding list will be valuable to users who none the less wish to note the subtle distinctions between the standard terms used in the present edition and the attendant 'translations' found in the previous edition — distinctions which were almost certainly not intended.

Finally, the new edition modernises the notational practice; this, together with the more generous layout, has much increased the legibility of Sevčík's exercises. Patent errors have been corrected, and all the written instructions have been re-drafted so that they may better reflect modern idiom in the languages represented.

MILLAN SACHANIA
Shepperton, England, 2000

PRÉFACE DE L'ÉDITEUR

Etablir une nouvelle édition d'une oeuvre qui est un classique dans son domaine est une tâche qu'on ne peut entreprendre à la légère. Un traité de technique aussi prestigieux que les études pour violon de Sevčík présente des défis particuliers. En le révisant, l'éditeur ne doit pas seulement considérer ses nouveaux utilisateurs potentiels, il lui revient également de ne causer ni embarras, ni inconfort inutiles à ses utilisateurs fidèles et expérimentés par son actualisation. Ceci suppose une approche équilibrée qui mêle innovation et tradition.

L'édition précédente, imprimée pour la première fois au début du vingtième siècle, manifestait des signes de vieillissement tant par son style de notation que par la qualité de sa gravure et de son graphisme. Néanmoins, sa longévité témoignait de la force de sa largeur de conception. Mon objectif a donc été d'en retenir les traits les plus attractifs et reconnus tout en corrigeant les défauts qui comprometaient son efficacité. En conséquence, la plupart des abréviations allemandes de l'édition précédente a été retenue. Quelques-unes ont toutefois été abandonnées au profit de la cohérence stylistique entre les volumes.

Dans sa quête de parité linguistique, l'ancienne édition donnait une traduction laborieuse à partir, généralement, de l'allemand vers l'anglais, le français, l'italien, le tchèque et le russe de nombreux termes définissant les styles de coups d'archet et de phrasé. (Assez curieusement, les termes italiens conventionnels tels que 'staccato' étaient maintenus dans les langues *autres* que l'italien, et remplacés par un autre mot italien ou une autre phrase dans les indications en italien.) Cette pratique non seulement encombrait le texte mais créait la confusion. En dépit de leur volonté certaine (confirmée par leur homogénéité) de fournir l'équivalent le plus proche dans chaque langue, ces 'traductions' comportaient parfois, et inévitablement, des nuances de sens différentes de celles présentes dans le concept original. Pour plus de clarté, notre édition recourt à la terminologie internationale conventionnelle. *Spiccato* figure sans l'équivalent allemand 'geworfen' ni le terme italien de 'sciolto balzato'; *jeté* sans les équivalents 'werfend', 'thrown', 'jerked', 'balzato', 'di rimbalzo'; *saltando* remplace 'springend', 'hopping', 'sautillé', 'saltellato', 'saltato'; *volante* remplace 'fliegend', 'flying', 'volant'; *martellato* remplace 'gehämmert', 'hammered', 'martelé'; et *staccato* remplace 'abgestoßen', 'chopped' et 'picchettato (secco)'. (L'ancienne édition confond par ailleurs parfois 'détaché' et 'staccato'.) La liste ci-dessus sera sans doute précieuse aux utilisateurs qui souhaiteraient néanmoins s'attacher aux distinctions subtiles existant entre les termes conventionnels utilisés dans cette édition et les 'traductions' équivalentes recontrées dans l'ancienne édition — distinctions qui n'avaient presque sûrement rien d'intentionnel.

Enfin, la notation de la nouvelle édition a été modernisée, ce qui, associé à une mise en page plus aérée, a beaucoup amélioré la lisibilité des exercices de Sevčík. Les erreurs évidentes ont été corrigées et toutes les indications écrites ont été re-rédigées de façon à refléter la forme actuelle des langues représentées.

MILLAN SACHANIA
Shepperton, Angleterre, 2000
Traduction: Agnès Ausseur

PREFAZIONE DELL'EDITORE

La preparazione di una nuova edizione di un'opera diventata oramai un classico nel suo campo, è un lavoro che non si puó intraprendere alla leggera. Un manuale di tecniche cosí prestigioso quanto quello per gli Studi del Violino di Ševčík puó presentare certe sue difficoltà. Nell'apportare le nuove modifiche, l'editore deve considerare non solo i nuovi e potenziali utenti dell'opera; esiste inoltre una responsabilità verso coloro che già sono a conoscenza degli esercizi, onde alleviare loro da qualsiasi difficoltà e rendere agevole la 'transizione' dalla vecchia alla nuova edizione. Questo richiede un approccio che sia equilibrato, cioè una revisione che unisca innovazione a conservatismo.

L'edizione precedente uscì per la prima volta in stampa agli inizi del ventesimo secolo. Tale edizione mostra segni di un'epoca passata, sia per lo stile della notazione musicale, che per la qualità di stampa ed immagine. Nonostante questo, la sua durabilità costituisce una testimonianza della solidità di una più ampia concezione. Il mio obbiettivo è stato quindi quello di ritenere le caratteristiche interessanti consolidate, eliminando quei difetti che ne riducevano la loro praticità. In conseguenza, la maggior parte delle abbreviazioni in tedesco sono state mantenute. Alcune, comunque, sono state eliminate nell'interesse di una consistenza stilistica tra i vari volumi.

Cercando di mantenere una parità linguistica, l'edizione precedente minuziosamente traduceva la maggior parte della terminologia denotando lo stile dei vari modi di esecuzione e articolazione. Generalmente, a incominciare col tedesco, venivano fornite le versioni equivalenti in inglese, francese, italiano, cecoslavacco e russo. (Stranamente però la vecchia edizione manteneva spesso termini standard in italiano quali 'staccato' nelle istruzioni date nella lingua *non* italiana; in questi casi le istruzioni date in italiano disponevano di una frase o di una parola alternativa.) Questa pratica servì non solo a rendere il testo troppo denso, ma anche a confondere. Peciò anche se l'intenzione era quella di dare il significato più vicino alla lingua in questione (supportata dalla consistenza delle 'traduzioni'), inevitabilmente le traduzioni davano a volte diverse sfumature di significato da quelle suggerite originariamente. Per maggior chiarezza, la presente edizione usa una traduzione standard della terminologia internazionale. *Spiccato* appare senza la corrispondente tedesca 'geworfen' e l'alternativa in italiano 'sciolto balzato'; *jeté*, senza la corrispondente 'werfend', 'thrown', 'jerked', 'balzato', 'di rimbalzo'; *saltando* sostituisce 'springend', 'hopping', 'sautillé', 'saltellato', 'saltato'; *volante* per 'fliegend', 'flying', 'volant'; *martellato* per 'gehämmert', 'hammered', 'martelé'; e *staccato* per 'abgestoßen', 'chopped' e 'picchettato (secco)'. (E' da notarsi che l'edizione precedente qualche volta confondeva 'detaché' con 'staccato'.) Senza dubbio la lista che precede sarà d'aiuto a coloro che nonostante tutto vogliono osservare attentamente le distinzioni tra i termini standard usati nella presente edizione e le rispettive 'traduzioni' trovate nell'edizione precedente — distinzioni che quasi sicuramente non erano volute.

Da ultimo, la nuova edizione aggiorna la pratica di notazione; questa, unita all'aspetto più largo della stampa, ha aumentato di molto la leggibilità degli esercizi di Ševčík. Sono stati corretti errori palesi ed il testo delle istruzioni è stato nuovamente redatto per meglio riflettere l'idioma moderno della lingua rappresentata.

MILLAN SACHANIA
Shepperton, Inghilterra, 2000
Traduzione: Anna Maggio

Anmerkung

Die vorliegenden Bogenübungen zerfallen in zwei Gruppen:
a) Übungen für den rechten Arm (Heft I und II)
b) Übungen für das Handgelenk (Heft III–VI)
Jede Gruppe bildet ein selbständiges und abgeschlossenes Ganzes;
doch erfordern beide Gruppen ein gleichzeitiges Studium, da die
Ausbildung des Armes parallel mit der Ausbildung des
Handgelenkes fortschreiten soll. Bei Nr. 5 des I. Heftes angelangt,
gehtes weiter im III. Heft, wo täglich einige Bogenstrichübungen
sowohl für den Arm als auch für das Handgelenk zu empfehlen
sind.

Introductory Note

The bowing exercises presented here are divided into two groups:
a) exercises for the right arm (Volumes I and II)
b) exercises for the wrist (Volumes III to VI)
Each group is independent and complete in itself, but, because the
arm and the wrist must be trained in parallel, the two groups should
be studied simultaneously. Thus the student should begin the
exercises contained in Volume III once No. 5 of Volume I has been
reached, so that the daily practice routine includes a few bowing
exercises for both the arm and the wrist.

Avertissement

Les exercices d'archet suivants se divisent en deux groupes:
a) exercices pour le bras droit (volumes I et II)
b) exercices pour le poignet (volumes III–VI)
Chaque groupe d'exercices forme un ensemble indépendant et
complet. Néanmoins, les deux groupes doivent être étudiés
simultanément de façon à développer en parallèle le travail du bras et
du poignet. On commencera les exercices du volume III dès que l'on
aura atteint l'exercice no. 5 du volume I. Le travail quotidien
comprendra ainsi des exercices d'archet à la fois pour le bras et pour
le poignet.

Nota

Gli esercizi qui illustrati si dividono in due gruppi:
a) esercizi per il braccio destro (Volumi I e II)
b) esercizi per il polso (Volumi III–VI)
Ogni gruppo di esercizi forma un'unità indipendente e compiuta;
i due gruppi devono comunque essere studiati insieme affinchè lo
sviluppo del braccio destro progredisca parallelemente con quello del
polso. Gli esercizi contenuti nella Volume III dovranno perciò essere
iniziati dopo aver raggiunto l'esercizio n. 5 della Volume I, in modo
che lo studio quotidiano includa esercizi di colpo d'arco sia per il
braccio, che per il polso.

Abkürzungen und Zeichen

G	Ganzer Bogen
H	Halber Bogen
uH	Untere Hälfte
oH	Obere Hälfte
1/3 B	Ein Drittel des Bogens
Fr	Am Frosch des Bogens
M	Mitte des Bogens
Sp	Spitze des Bogens
M*	In der Mitte, dann an der Spitze und am Frosch
⊓	Abstrich †
∨	Aufstrich
–	Breit stoßen ‡
·	*Staccato* oder *martellato*
∨	*Jeté, spiccato* oder *saltando*
)	Bogen heben

† Wenn am Anfang einer Übung kein Zeichen beigesetzt ist, so fängt die erste Note immer am Frosch im Abstrich an.

‡ Noten, über denen kein Bogenstrich gesetzt ist, werden gestoßen gespielt.

Abréviations et signes

G	Tout l'archet
H	Moitié de l'archet
uH	Moitié inférieure
oH	Moitié supérieure
1/3 B	Tiers de l'archet
Fr	Du talon de l'archet
M	Du milieu de l'archet
Sp	De la pointe de l'archet
M*	Du milieu, puis de la pointe et du talon de l'archet
⊓	Tiré †
∨	Poussé
–	Détaché large ‡
·	*Staccato* ou *martellato*
∨	*Jeté, spiccato* ou *saltando*
)	Lever l'archet

† S'il n'y a pas de signe au début d'un exercice, on attaque toujours la première note du talon en tirant.

‡ En l'absence d'indication de phrasé, on détache toutes les notes.

Abbreviations and Symbols

G	Whole bow
H	Half bow
uH	Lower half of bow
oH	Upper half of bow
1/3 B	Third of bow
Fr	Heel of bow
M	Middle of bow
Sp	Point of bow
M*	In the middle of the bow, and then at the point and at the heel
⊓	Down-bow †
∨	Up-bow
–	Broadly detached ‡
·	*Staccato* or *martellato*
∨	*Jeté, spiccato* or *saltando*
)	Raise the bow from the string

† If no sign is shown at the beginning of an exercise, the first note should be begun at the heel, with a down-bow.

‡ Where there is no such articulation, each note should be detached.

Abbreviazioni e Segni

G	Tutto l'arco
H	Metà dell'arco
uH	Metà inferiore dell'arco
oH	Metà superiore dell'arco
1/3 B	Un terzo dell'arco
Fr	Tallone
M	Mezzo dell'arco
Sp	Punta dell'arco
M*	Nel mezzo, poi sulla punta e sul tallone
⊓	In giù †
∨	In su
–	Staccato lungo ‡
·	Staccato o martellato
∨	*Jeté,* spiccato o saltando
)	Alzare l'arco

† Se all'inizio di un esercizio non c'e nessun segno, s'incomincia sempre la prima nota col tallone (in giù).

‡ Bisogna staccare tutte le note di cui non è indicato il colpo d'arco.

2

No. 13

Etüde in Triolen mit 105 Varianten des Bogenstriches. Dieselbe auf der 7. Lage. (Siehe Nr. 26.)

Study in triplets, with 105 changes of bowing style. Also to be practised in 7th position (see No. 26).

Etude en triolets avec 105 changements de coups d'archet. Voir au No. 26 la même étude sur la 7e position.

Studio di terzine con 105 cambiamenti di colpi d'arco. Da eseguire anche nella 7^a posizione (vedi N. 26).

Stricharten / Bowing styles
Coups d'archet / Colpi d'arco

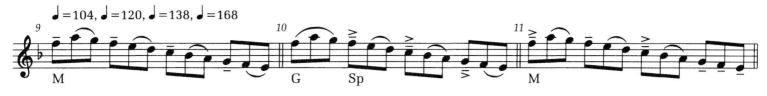

4

Staccato picchiettato

Spiccato

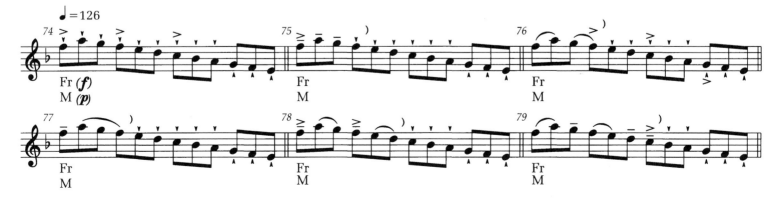

Cresc. / Dim.

No. 14

Etüde in Triolen (3/4 Takt) mit 77 Varianten des Bogenstriches. Dieselbe auf der 4. Lage. (Siehe Nr. 25.)

Study in triplets in 3/4 time, with 77 changes of bowing style. Also to be practised in 4th position (see No. 25).

Etude en triolets (mesure à 3/4) avec 77 changements de coups d'archet. Voir au No. 25 la même étude sur la 4e position.

Studio di terzine (battuta in 3/4) con 77 cambiamenti di colpi d'arco. Da eseguire anche nella 4^a posizione (vedi N. 25).

Stricharten / Bowing styles
Coups d'archet / Colpi d'arco

Spiccato

8

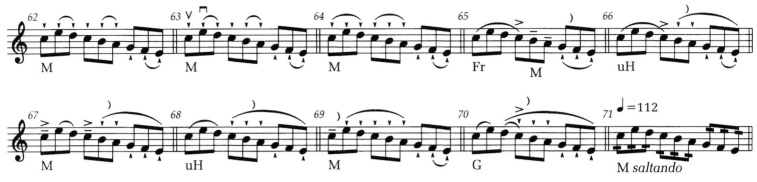

No. 15

Etüde in Sechzehnteln (6/8 Takt) mit 64 Varianten des Bogenstriches. Dieselbe auf der 4. Lage. (Siehe Nr. 27.)

Study in semiquavers in 6/8 time, with 64 changes of bowing style. Also to be practised in 4th position (see No. 27).

Etude en doubles croches (mesure à 6/8) avec 64 changements de coups d'archet. Voir au No. 27 la même étude sur la 4e position.

Studio di semicrome (battuta in 6/8) con 64 cambiamenti di colpi d'arco. Da eseguire anche nella 4^a posizione (vedi N. 27).

9

Stricharten / Bowing styles
Coups d'archet / Colpi d'arco

détaché

Spiccato

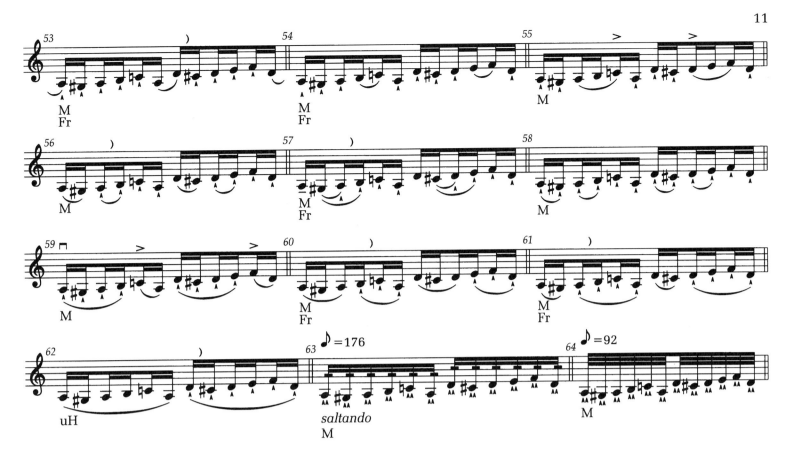

No. 16

Etüde in Sechzehnteln (3/4 Takt) mit 68 Varianten des Bogenstriches.	Study in semiquavers in 3/4 time, with 68 changes of bowing style.	Etude en doubles croches (mesure à 3/4) avec 68 changements de coups d'archet.	Studio di semicrome (battuta in 3/4) con 68 cambiamenti di colpi d'arco.

Allegro moderato

12

Stricharten / Bowing styles
Coups d'archet / Colpi d'arco

Spiccato

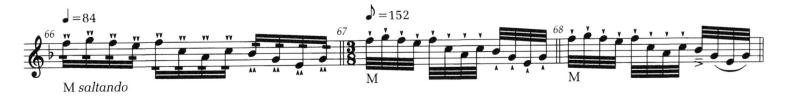

14

No. 17

Etüde in Sechzehnteln (4/4 Takt) mit 131 Varianten des Bogenstriches. Dieselbe in der 5. Lage. (Siehe Nr. 28.)

Study in semiquavers in 4/4 time, with 131 changes of bowing style. Also to be practised in 5th position (see No. 28).

Etude en double croches (mesure à 4/4) avec 131 changements de coups d'archet. Voir au No. 28 la même étude sur la 5e position.

Studio di semicrome (battuta in 4/4) con 131 cambiamenti di colpi d'arco. Da eseguire anche nella 5^a posizione (vedi N. 28).

Stricharten / Bowing styles
Coups d'archet / Colpi d'arco

† Die zweite Takthälfte ebenso wie die erste.

† The two halves of the bar should be played in exactly the same way.

† Les deux moitiés de la mesure seront jouées exactement de la même façon.

† Le due metà delle battute dovrebbero essere eseguite esattamente nella stessa maniera.

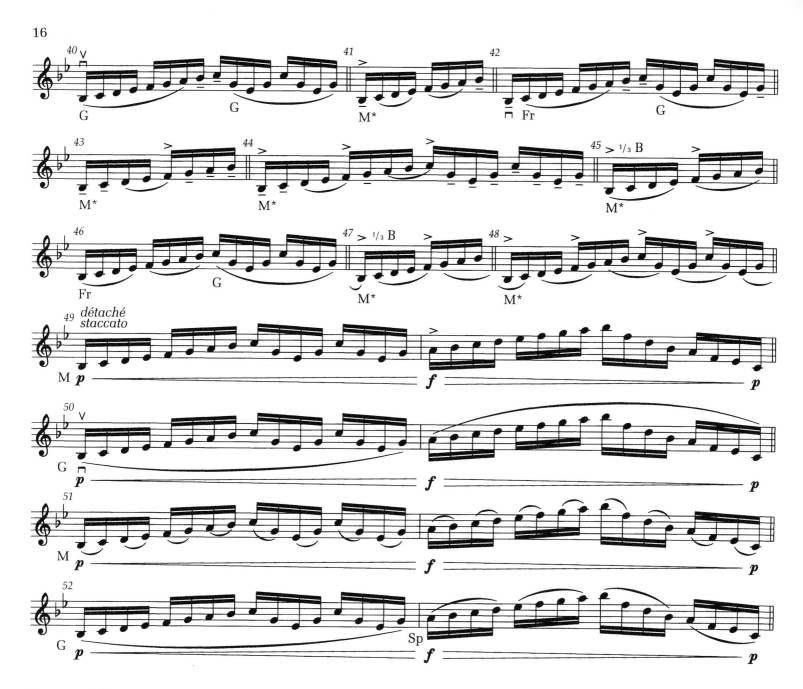

Staccato picchiettato

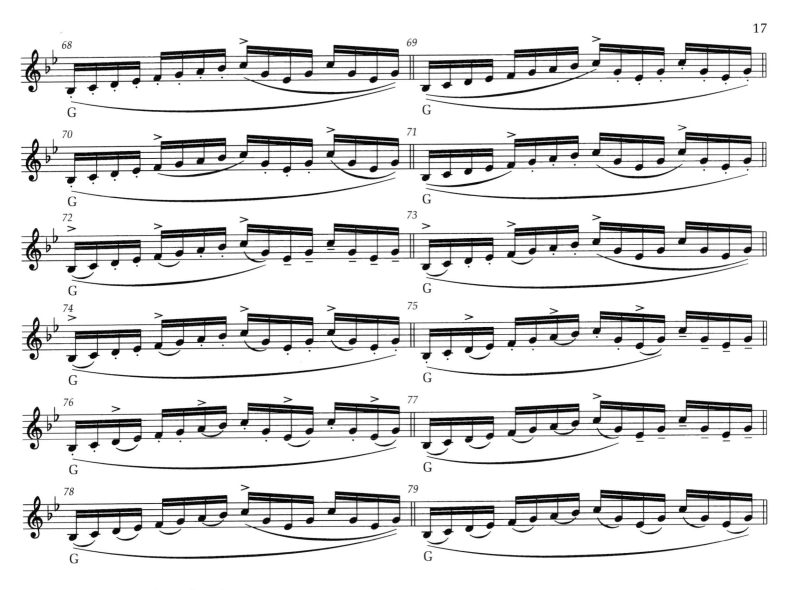

Punktierte Sechzehntel / Dotted semiquavers
Doubles croches pointées / Semicrome puntate

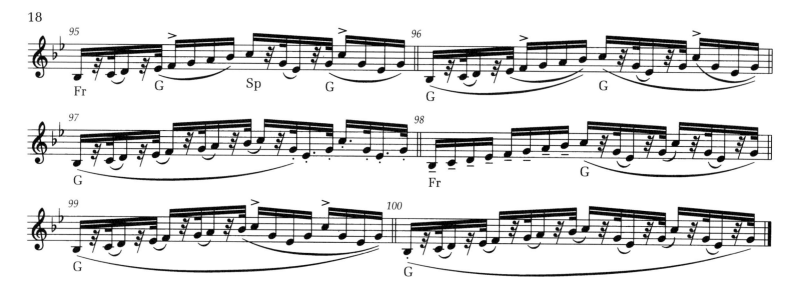

Spiccato

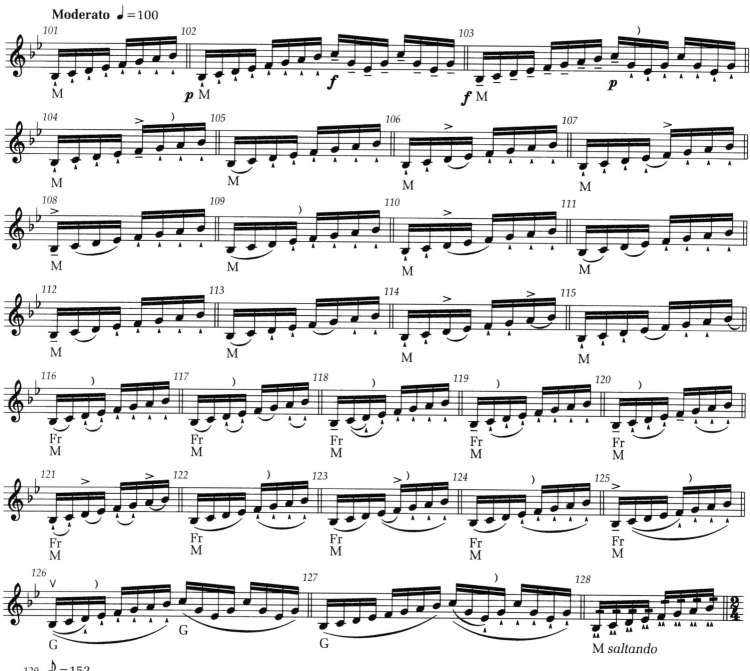

| Übungen im *pp* am Griffbrett für die Ausbildung der Weichheit des Tones. | Exercises in *pp* over the fingerboard, in order to develop softness of tone. | Exercices en *pp* sur la touche pour développer la douceur du son. | Esercizi suonando *pp* sulla tastiera per sviluppare la dolcezza del suono. |

No. 18

| Beispiel mit 30 Varianten | Example, with 30 variants | Exemple et 30 variantes | Esempio con 30 varianti |

Andante ♩=69
3. Lage / 3rd Pos.

sempre **pp** *sulla tastiera*
2. viol.

Varianten | **Variants** | **Variantes** | **Varianti**

Mit ganzem Bogen / Whole bow
Tout l'archet / Tutto l'arco

Mit halbem Bogen / Half-bow
Moitié de l'archet / Metà dell'arco

Mit halbem und ganzem Bogen / With half and whole bow
Moitié de l'archet et tout l'archet / Metà dell'arco e tutto l'arco

Mit der Mitte des Bogens / Middle of bow
Du milieu de l'archet / Col mezzo dell'arco

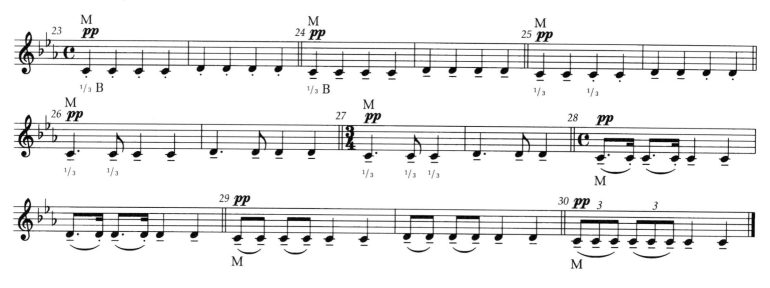

No. 19

Fortsetzung der Übungen im *pp* am Griffbrett. Etüde mit 59 Varianten.	Exercises in *pp* over the fingerboard (continued). Study, with 59 variants.	Exercices en *pp* sur la touche (suite). Etude et 59 variantes.	Esercizi suonando *pp* sulla tastiera (seguito). Studio con 59 varianti.

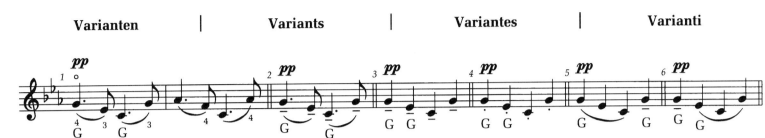

Varianten | Variants | Variantes | Varianti

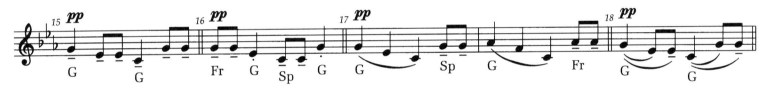

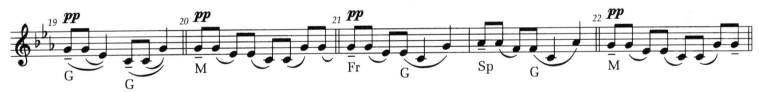

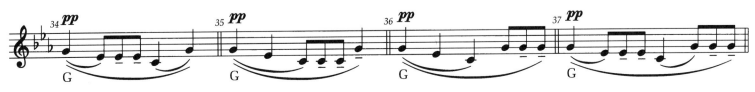

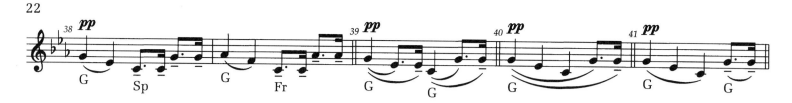

No. 20

Übung in gehaltenen Tönen und im Zurückhalten des Bogens.	Study in sustained notes, for economising the bow.	Exercice de sons filés et de retenue de l'archet.	Esercizi di note prolungate per un uso economico dell'arco.
Die vorhergehenden Etüden Nr 3–7 und 13–17 sind auf folgende Arten zu üben:	Practise exercises 3–7 and 13–17 with the following bowing:	On travaillera les études précédentes Nos 3–7 et 13–17 en liant les mesures des manières suivantes:	Esercitarsi sugli studi precedenti dai N. 3–7 e da 13–17 legando le battute nelle maniere seguenti:
a) Zu 2 Takten unter einem Bogenstrich, *f*	a) 2 bars with one bow stroke, *f*	a) par 2 mesures du même coup d'archet en *f*	a) 2 battute con lo stesso colpo d'arco suonando *f*
b) Zu 4 Takten unter einem Bogenstrich, *p*	b) 4 bars with one bow stroke, *p*	b) par 4 mesures du même coup d'archet en *p*	b) 4 battute con lo stesso colpo d'arco suonando *p*
c) Zu 8 Takten unter einem Bogenstrich, *ppp*	c) 8 bars with one bow stroke, *ppp*	c) par 8 mesures du même coup d'archet en *ppp*	c) 8 battute con lo stesso colpo d'arco suonando *ppp*

| **Beispiele** | **Examples** | **Exemples** | **Esempi** |

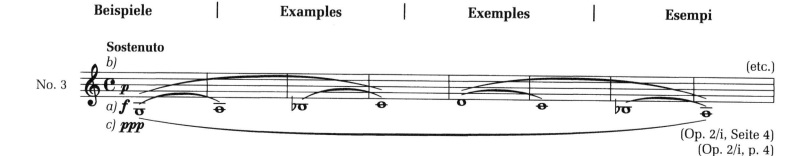

(Op. 2/i, Seite 4)
(Op. 2/i, p. 4)

No. 4 — Andante — *p f* — *ppp* — (etc.)

(Op. 2/i, Seite 6)
(Op. 2/i, p. 6)

No. 5 — Moderato — *p f* — *ppp* — (etc.)

(Op. 2/i, Seite 9)
(Op. 2/i, p. 9)

No. 7 — Allegretto — *p f* — *ppp* — (etc.)

(etc.)

(Op. 2/i, Seite 24)
(Op. 2/i, p. 24)

No. 6 — Allegro moderato — *p f* — *ppp* — (etc.)

(etc.)

(Op. 2/i, Seite 18)
(Op. 2/i, p. 18)

No. 14 — Allegro — *p f* — *ppp* — (etc.)

(etc.)

(Op. 2/ii, Seite 6)
(Op. 2/ii, p. 6)

24

Übungen in gebrochenen Akkorden auf 3 und 4 Saiten mit Anwendung der vorhergehenden Stricharten.	Arpeggio exercises over 3 and 4 strings, using bowing styles from preceding exercises.	Exercices en accords brisés sur 3 et 4 cordes utilisant les exercices d'archet précédents.	Esercizi di accordi arpeggiati sopra 3 e 4 corde applicandovi gli esercizi di colpi d'arco precedenti.

No. 21

Mit Stricharten 1–97 aus Nr. 13.	With the bowings of variants 1–97 of No. 13.	Avec les coups d'archet 1 à 97 du No. 13.	Con colpi d'arco 1–97 del N. 13.

No. 22

Mit Stricharten aus Nr. 16.	With the bowings of No. 16.	Avec les coups d'archet du No. 16.	Con colpi d'arco del N. 16.

No. 23

Mit Stricharten aus Nr. 17. | With the bowings of No. 17. | Avec les coups d'archet du No. 17. | Con colpi d'arco del N. 17.

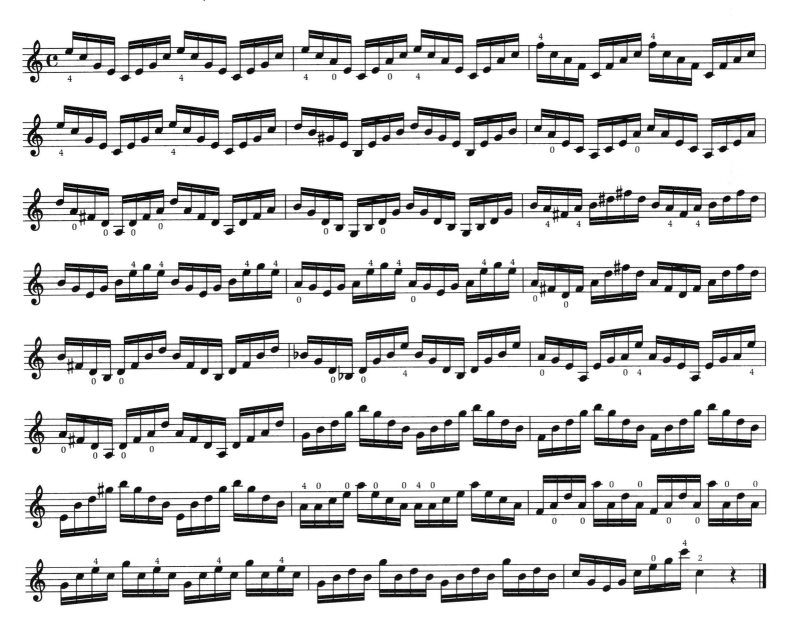

26

No. 24

Mit Stricharten aus Nr. 15. | With the bowings of No. 15. | Avec les coups d'archet du No. 15. | Con colpi d'arco del N. 15.

Anwendung der vorhergehenden Bogenübungen auf hohen Lagen: | The preceding bowing exercises in the high positions: | Exercices précédents dans les positions élevées: | Gli esercizi d'arco precedenti nelle posizioni superiori:

No. 25

Mit Stricharten aus Nr. 14. | With the bowings of No. 14. | Avec les coups d'archet du No. 14. | Con colpi d'arco del N. 14.

4. Lage / 4th position
4e position / 4^a posizione

No. 26

Mit Stricharten aus Nr. 13. | With the bowings of No. 13. | Avec les coups d'archet du No. 13. | Con colpi d'arco del N. 13.

7. Lage / 7th position
7^e position / 7^a posizione

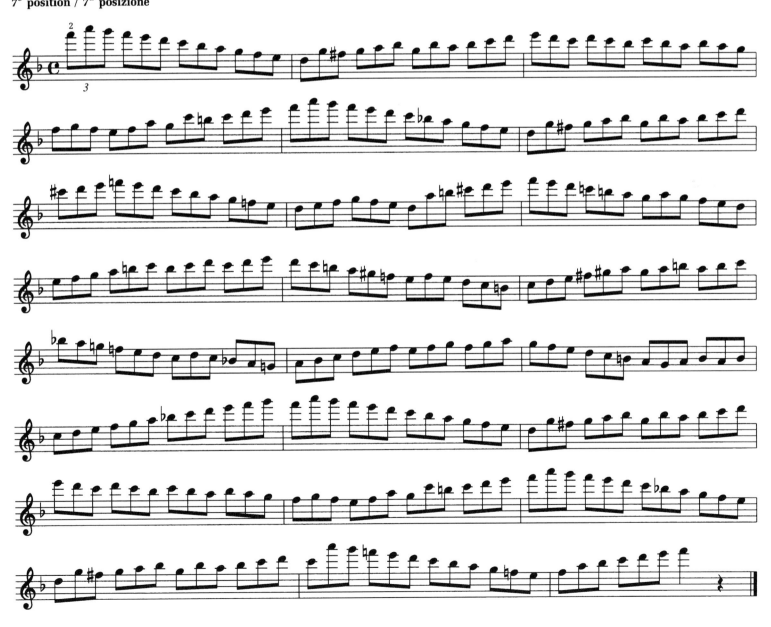

28

No. 27

Mit Stricharten aus Nr. 15. | With the bowings of No. 15. | Avec les coups d'archet du No. 15. | Con colpi d'arco del N. 15.

4. Lage / 4th position
4^e position / 4^a posizione

No. 28

Mit Stricharten aus Nr. 17. | With the bowings of No. 17. | Avec les coups d'archet du No. 17. | Con colpi d'arco del N. 17.

5. Lage / 5th position
5^e position / 5^a posizione

Typeset by Musonix